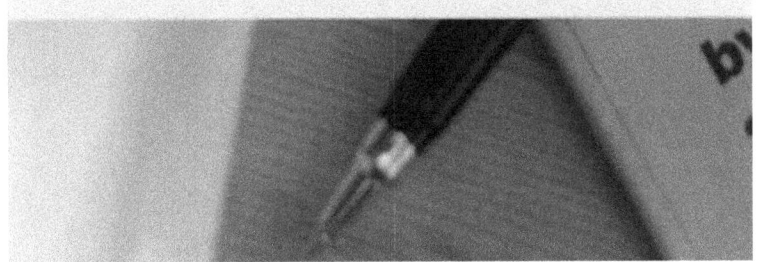

Strange Questions,
Even Stranger Answers
Prophetess Tina Seals

Strange Questions, Even Stranger Answers
Written by Prophetess Tina Seals

{This page left blank intentionally}

Strange Questions, Even Stranger Answers

Written by
Prophetess Tina Seals

Table of Contents

Strange Questions, Even Stranger Answers
Written by Prophetess Tina Seals

Copyright

Tina Seals Books & Publishing

http://www.tinaseals.net

http://www.tinaseals.com

Seals_tina@yahoo.com

tina@tinaseals.net

tina@tinaseals.com

Strange Questions, Even Stranger Answers
Written by Prophetess Tina Seals

Dedication

This book is dedicated to all of you, my Grand Jury fans!

Be blessed as you read –

Prophetess Tina Seals

About This Book

In all humor, and sincerity, please find the following, as an answer to "A Grand Jury".

Perhaps if you read it with this understanding, you will understand the random nature, of the content, provided here today!

Thanks.

Prophetess Tina Seals

Understanding How the Book Is Written

Of course, based on the "About This Book" section, you realize that this book is not a "typical read".

Meaning, it's not going to make sense to you, as far as "flow" and all of that "readability" stuff goes, if you don't realize, off the top, that the nature of the book, is "interrogatory" by nature.

It's basically comprised of text that answers questions. So please keep that in mind as you read.

Because there is extreme randomness, from page to page. The topics are not interwoven.

I'm simply answering the questions that I believe, you need additional clarity on.

It's important for you to realize this, or you will get lost, in the flow of the book, thinking it to have a hidden meaning, that is non-existent.

I'm saying everything I wanted to say. And there is no hidden agenda to this writing. It doesn't have a hidden message, or its not code for something else.

Can you rape your spouse?

My answer to this question is "Yes". Because there are a few things one must consider, when they consider both "the status of the marriage", the "authenticity of the marriage", "knowledge of the marriage", and "marital consent". So yes, I do believe one has the capacity to rape a "spouse".

The question then becomes, why a wife or husband, would feel "raped" or "violated", in the first place?

Do they know they are married to the person sexing their body?

Does the person who is being intimate with them, drug, and then rape them? Without both consent, and knowledge?

Was the marriage license obtained fraudulently?

Is the wife a mail order bride?

Why would the other spouse feel "violated" by "sexual intimacy" with their "spouse", if they consented to marriage, in the first place?

The question then becomes, the validation and proof that actual marriage, in both legality, and relationship, really exists!

I believe the solution to the whole "legal question" of "marital rape", lies in getting the "married couple" together, and asking both of them, before legal professionals, and law enforcement, if one or both of them, feels "violated", by the sexual interaction of the other.

Instead of constantly debating the "rape your spouse" question, let's start debating, "how valid is your marriage" question!

Let's begin that process right now!

Get both parties together, in front of law enforcement, so either can be arrested, if needed. And begin asking the important questions.

When did you meet?

How did you meet?

Who introduced you?

Where did you meet?

Where was your first date? Sexual encounter? Did you enjoy it? Do you want to be in relationship with this individual?

Do you share kids?

Do you know his mother? Father? Sisters? Brothers?

What is his middle name?

What is his last name?

What is his date of birth?

Where was he born?

What was the last purchase you made together?

When was the last time you took a trip together?

Where is your home?

Do you own rental or other property?

How much money do you have in the bank?

When was the last time you went to the doctor for a physical checkup? And your spouse?

What medical conditions does your spouse have?

Which ones do you have?

Show me your marriage license!

Then, after you ask all of these questions, give both a lie detector test. And test their children for semen in the ass.

Then begin to have the very important discussion about how its illegal to racket, traffick human DNA, embryos, eggs, and then attempt to cover it, extort, blackmail, take hostages, and lie under oath!

And then ask, one more time, "Do you feel violated, under such circumstance, to have sexual intercourse, with your "SPOUSE"?

Are You Russian?

The next strange question, I often get, and am very excited about addressing is: "Are you Russian?"

My answer to that "very strange" question is, "Are you?"

Go ask Mikael Gorbachev, he should know.

Did you find my Russian birth certificate? And if so, when can I get deported.

Next, can you give me lessons in Russian, because I am going to need to speak the language, once I get there?

Also, who the hell brought me, a Russian national, to America?

And then, I will ask, "Are you Russian?"

Maybe the "Russians" put something in my laundry, or walked by, real fast, when the sniffing dog, full of shit, ran by, and thought I was "Russian".

Again, I ask, "Are you Russian?"

Who Are You Voting For? And Why?

A conservative. Because Wall Street, and the operations, that generate commerce, run off of the health and well-being of Wall Street. So it's important to elect a legislator who understands business, and how to restore financial institutions, banks, and the operations of trade, in this nation.

Will You Ever Vote For Hillary?

No. Because the last time I tried to support her campaign, she acted arrogantly towards me. She somehow believed that I wanted face time with her.

I don't know Hillary. And I don't want to know Hillary. And I pray I never meet her either.

She can stay in Washington, in the congress, and do what she does.

I think she is a great lawmaker. Nothing against her in that way. But I think it is tragic for constituents, to be made to feel, as "stalkers", or "harassers", because they get excited about a candidate's campaign.

When she improperly labeled me, as one or both of those, I let her go.

She will never, ever, ever, ever, ever, ever, times a million, to infinity, ever, have to worry about me ever, supporting anything she does.

I am over Ms. Hillary Clinton.

Smile.

Do I Want to Meet Barack Obama?

No. I have no need to meet him. I see him on TV and that's enough for me.

I think he is doing a great job with the nation. And I think he has overcome insurmountable odds, and challenges, to accomplish the great things, he has, but I have no desire to meet him, or work for him.

What Is My Dream Job?

My dream job is singing, and preaching the gospel around the world. And I will pursue that, once I get housed, and have a steady income, coming in, so that I don't have to beg for money on the street, or live in a homeless shelter.

Why Do You Want to Be A Police Officer?

I don't. I like going home at night. And it is against my religion to carry a weapon, fight, or engage myself in illegal activities. I will leave that to the real police out there.

For me, being in a shelter and all, I needed a means to an end. I needed a way out of the shelter system. I needed a paycheck on Friday. So I took Civil Service Exams, so that I could get a job.

I had no idea the Civil Service process was so intricate, or took so long.

And DCAS sucks. They don't work with the Police Department to coordinate anything. I missed two appointments, because of the negligence of DCAS. Luckily, I just received a letter in the mail, to report for work, with NYPD Traffic section, on Thursday, the 30th, 2015.

So I am excited about that!

Police jobs were, basically, the only jobs being offered at the time, when I took the Civil Service Exam. And they had a couple of welfare jobs too, of course. I applied for those as well, but didn't pass those test. But I got a 94% on Traffic, and a 84% on Special Officer. That test is like for working in a shelter, or library, as a non-commissioned, security guard.

I also applied for a Security Guard license. Its not so much my desire to be in law enforcement. Its that I have been the victim of identity theft, and needed to work, despite that. And so, because police, and security jobs, check your background, it was easy for me to get that type of work. They know I am clear, background wise, because they check it!

Other public companies are not so security intelligent. They don't know if my background is clear or not. So if they suspect that I was the other person, who has criminal issues, they would just block the processing of my application.

The police won't do that because they know I am clear, and eligible to work.

How Many Kids Do I Have?

Three that I gave birth to. And of course, a few that I am god-mother to.

But for the most part, just three. I made a decision to give birth to three: Alex, Robert, Antonio.

Am I Married?

Laugh. This question is always difficult to answer. Because if I say no, I might be wrong. Laugh.

And I hear you say, "What?"

No but for real, if I say, I'm not married, I might be wrong.

And I would be wrong, about that if:

- Someone married me without my consent, permission, or knowledge

But if you ask me, "Have you chosen to marry within the last 20 years, or so?" I would have to say, "No. I have no dated in the last 20 years, so I know, I don't have any marital prospects, from the last 20 years."

And please notice, I placed that in quotations for you, so you can cut and paste it, into whatever document, you desire to put it into!

Now, even though I'm not married, legally, with knowledge, based on knowledge, and consent, I will say this. If a certain man, asked me to marry, or married me on paper, I wouldn't be offended. I would just want to know.

But in the kingdom of God, this is not the way things are supposed to happen!

What Is Your Race?

I have no clue. I know I am black, some sort of black, and a mix of something other.

I think when they did an assessment on me, because the feds were searching, so they could deport me, because of the Human Traffick, they determined that I was African, Jamaican, and Native American.

I'm okay with that.

As far as culture goes, I grew up in African American culture, and consider myself African American.

And, when they put the blue light on me, I turn dark black. When they shine the red light on me, I turn medium to dark brown, my oldest son's color. And when they shine the yellow light on me, I look like a dark Dominican.

I think the green light makes me look African as well.

And I am 100% okay with being African, and dark skinned.

I know it baffles many that my skin, gets so dark, under the lights. But that is how black folk are.

Only God can explain that!

Do You Know Anyone Named Dillan?

No. Not really. I mean, I was introduced to a bassist, at City College in 2013, who studied upright bass. But other than that, I have never met anyone named "Dillan", or "Villain".

Do You Have Any White Kids?

Nope. None.

Do You Have Any Other Race of children, Besides Black?

No. Never chose to brand myself in that manner.

Don't date outside of the black, African American race.

I'm not interested in that. At all!

Do You Own Pets?

No.

Have You Ever Owned Pets?

Yes. I had one white dog. He was a mutt. A lab and street dog, mix breed. And he had worms. A kid sold him to me, back in 96, at a Kroger grocery store, in Houston.

I tried to make him happy but he cried all the time. I didn't realize it was because he had worms, and because he was too young to be separate from his mom.

But I had a Caucasian lady, living next door, who was good with animals. And I gave her the dog. And she had him for about a week, and he grew to be tall and beautiful.

Will You Ever Have Another Dog?

I don't know. Black folks don't think that's too sanitary! We don't usually have pets. Unless we are extremely wealthy, and can keep the pet up properly.

Most black folks, and I am generalizing, don't consider pets, family. So we don't let them sleep in the bed, and eat at the table, or mate with us.

And the bible teaches against such practices as well.

Are You Muslim?

Definitely not. I don't have a problem with Muslims, but I am not one.

Nor do I believe in the principles of Islam. Although, I do realize that many believe Islam, to be older than Christianity. And in many ways, that is true.

Because Christianity, as an organized religion, wasn't documented, in the Roman Empire, until after, Christ came to earth, the first time.

So although, Christianity, as Christians believe, is from Eternity, before the system of time, as far as documentation goes, and shows, it appears to have hit earth, after Islam.

But no. I am not Islamic, or Muslim.

I do not participate in Ramadan, or other Islamic events.

And I don't have anything against those who do, but that is not for me.

Do You Believe the White Man Is A Devil?

Yes. Laugh. And laugh again. I believe all men are devils. And all women, for that matter.

Laugh.

And I believe the remedy to that, is that they all, including myself, need to be Born Again, as Christianity, teaches.

Are You From Africa?

I pray so. I pray the Department of State finds a definitive birth record for me, and deports be back to South Africa!

Oh God, how I pray they do!

I feel like there is a chance I could have met Mr. Mandela, in another life. And actually have been in Africa, and traveled through Africa.

But, no, as far as I know, I don't know that I have traveled Africa. But I do feel that I have. Smile. And I sure can't wait to travel Africa!

You know, all blacks have some historical point of reference in Africa. So to say, I am not African, is a lie.

In my heart, I would like to believe, I am from a French Colony, in Africa!

Are You Anti-US Government?

No. Of course not. I think the US Government is awesome! When it works properly, that is!

I have to tell you, when you all, and speaking mainly of congress here, were cutting people off of Unemployment, back in 2011, I saw those dirty moves you made, and I was ashamed of you.

You should have been ashamed of yourself. You guys timed out so many Unemployment Clams, by withholding "extension approvals" for a week, or day, and forced so many claimants, off of Unemployment. I thought that was dirty as heck!

And then, if that wasn't dirty enough, I watched you lie, and say, "Oh, the Unemployment rate went down!"

Really? It did? No it didn't!

What you should have said, or meant to say was: "Unemployment numbers went down, because welfare numbers went up! We ingeniously ended the claims of over 200 million families, and forced them into the "no-income bracket", by making them ineligible for any more extensions, under Unemployment Law".

That is what you meant to say, but I know you got the PR Comments mixed up.

But don't worry. Because the next time I see you pull a dirty move like that, I am going to pay for radio time, to call you out!

But yeah, I think the government is good.

I must admit however, I am so turned off with Congress, as are most Americans. I do think they have gotten a whole lot better, since 2011. But they are still full of it!

I would never run for office though! And I mean that with all of my heart! Some of yawl are full of it, and corrupt as they come!

But I do like the government.

I am pro-government. And I believe in a large Central Unit!

Why Are You Studying Political Science

Because I was finished my AAS Paralegal, at Laguardia Community college in Dec. of 2010, and moved on to study music at City College of New York.

But before I went there, I started in 2011 at John Jay. And I see now, I should have just graduated from John Jay. Because it's a fair institution. And it is top notch for Police Science, and Government Science.

But I didn't know that then.

So now, here, in 2015, I'm still in need of 15 to 30 credits, for my Bachelors, at 44 years old, and I am looking to complete it, at John Jay.

I should have never transferred from John Jay, to City College. That is where all of my identity theft problems occurred.

And I had to deal with a whole lot of garbage in the Music Department, over there, under Dr. Jablonsky's leadership.

Although he was very kind to me, some of his staff, were devils. And they did everything they could to harass, deter, and negativity label me.

But anyway, that nightmare is over. I will never set foot in that demonic institution, ever again. I will package my degree over here at John Jay, and go on to Law School – God say the same!

But I started in Political Science, because a great professor, at City College, and another, in Law, saved me from the Publishing and Music, hate.

Dr. Bruce Cronin, and Dr. Timothy Porter, both took me under their instruction, after they saw me being unjustly persecuted, at City. They kind of helped me weather the storm, summer of 2013, into fall of 2013, at which time I ended up leaving the school.

So, it wasn't that I wanted to work in Government, or Political Science. It was that I wanted to get a music degree, as a humanity degree, for the purposes of having a well-rounded education to support entry to Law School.

After the music degree fell through, they advised me to take Political Science. They instructed that Law Schools like to see either Political Science, Public Administration, or a Humanity Degree, for entering Law Students.

And it also made sense, after reviewing my transcript, because a lot of the courses from my Associates, at LAGCC, fit into the Political Science degree.

I wanted to get a Law Degree, after the music fell through, but I was informed that a Law Degree, is not desired by Law Schools, but rather a

Humanity Degree. As they want students to have a well-rounded education.

And it would have been a bit too much work for me to major in English, or Creative Writing. So I chose Political Science.

Where Do You See Yourself In Five Years?

In a new home, working full-time, in ministry, and music. Possibly living in South Africa, or some other country, south of France.

I see myself successfully published, and making moves, professionally, in music (Gospel), and ministry.

Why Do You Want to Live Abroad?

I don't consider it abroad. I consider it a return to my motherland. My country. The place where I belong. That is where I want to be. I want to influence my people. I want to bring wealth back to the country. I want to feed and clothe the poor. I want to create intellectuals that can assist in changing the economic demographics of the country.

Nelson is gone. We need new leaders to rise up, and continue to build the nation, and leadership in our people.

I want to do that. That is my heart's desire.

I want to live in South Africa.

When Do You Want To Go To Africa?

I would leave today, if I could! I would be on the next international flight to Africa, today, if I could!

You Would Leave your Kids?

Alex, Robert, and Tonio, can go to Africa with me, if they like. Smile. That would be cool!

Is Your Mother Black?

Yes. 100% African American. Whatever that "black she is comprised of" – is.

And so is the rest of my family. And so am I. So are my kids.

Do You Speak Any Languages?

No. Not really. I speak some street Spanish that I learned from living in Washington Heights. And I learned a little French, from LAGCC. But I really don't speak any other language, fluently, besides American English.

Can You Understand Any Other Languages?

No. Laugh. But I laugh, because, now that I have had to ask for dollars, on the streets of New York, I have come to learn a little Spanish. So now, when people speak to me, who only speak Spanish, I can get the general idea, of what they are trying to say, even if I don't understand the full message.

Do You Believe In Spanking Kids?

Um. No. Not really. That's a tough question though. Because the bible, which I believe in, and live by, teaches that we are to use discipline, to correct our children, including spanking. But I personally, don't do it.

I tapped the leg of one of my kids when he was a boy, and it hurt me, more than it did him. I don't believe in hitting kids, because I was abused, as a kid.

So that's probably why I don't spank kids.

Besides that, kids are intelligent enough to know, and understand, when you tell them not to do something.

I think spanking and hollering at kids, breaks their spirit. For a long time I had a broken spirit as a kid, from being mishandled, or abused, as a kid.

I would never want to inflict that pain upon my kids, or other kids.

But I know other Christians don't feel the way I feel. And that is cool. To each his or her own.

But let me say, there is a clear definition, biblically, and otherwise, regarding discipline by spanking. And it is never equal to abuse, or disciplining a child in frustration, rage, violence, or anger. That is child abuse. Just call it what it is!

Anytime you handle a child with violence of any kind, you are operating in child abuse. This includes sexual, physical, mental, or emotional.

Why not go pick on someone your own size, you jerk!

What Do You Think of Your Leader(s)?

Wow. That's a strange question.

I mean, what should I think of them?

Laugh.

I see them as leaders to my life.

I view them as strength to me, as I move to varied levels of success.

I don't know. I don't know how to answer that.

But clearly, in my mind, there is always a line, between myself, and my leadership.

I don't consider myself on their level. And, I would never disrespect them, and put myself on their level.

I have no authority in my church, if that is what you are asking.

And I don't want any. I am perfectly happy being a pew member, or singing in the choir.

Smile.

I used to think I wanted to pastor, one day. But then I saw all the stuff, my leaders go through. And thought, "Naw, I don't want to do that!"

I will say this, I am grateful for my leaders. I have learned a great deal from them. And I thank God, daily, that they chose to say yes to God, and serve.

Do You See Yourself As a Leader?

Yes.   But not in Congress.   Not in Government. Not over a church. And not at PFC.

I see myself a leader, in my life. I see myself a leader by the good life I live, before those, who need an example.

I see myself as a leader to my children.

I see myself as a leader to the world, when I preach, sing, and do prophetic things.

That is the extent of my leadership skills.

If I Could Have Dinner With Anyone Living Or Dead?

I don't know. Years prior, I would have said Oprah, or Whitney.

And I might have a few days ago, said my pastor, or Bishop Jakes.

But now, I think I can have dinner with myself, and be perfectly happy!

I like me.

And let me say, I have changed. My life has changed. I have been so tremendously hurt, and humiliated, by this trial, and grand jury violence, that I don't want to interact with anyone, but God, and myself.

I think, albeit extremely painful, almost to the point of tears, at times, it has taught me a valuable lesson.

It has taught me that God's love never dies. And that God loves me. And that God is really all I have. And all I need. And all I want.

And of course, it has taught me that making money is important, after serving God, of course.

And it has taught me that I want to be financially secure, wealthy, and independently wealthy, so I can do the things I love to do!

What Are Your Goals?

Well, my first goal is to become gainfully employed, in a secular job. Because I tried to become gainfully employed by preaching, and or singing, and that didn't work for me.

So I have come to realize that I still need to work a job, in order to have housing, and take care of myself properly. Then, after I fix that, I can address taking my craft – music, and books – to the next level.

But I have to use balance, because I am 44, and not getting any younger.

But I do have definite goals, plans, and desires, for the long-term, and immediate future.

I also pray to attend and graduate, with honors, Law School. But of course, I must first, finish my bachelors, and I still have a $5k bursar stop from City College of New York.

So the job is important, so that I can finish up my degree by Dec. of 2015, and go ahead and apply for Law School, and move forward with my goals.

Do You Want To Date?

No. Not really.

I just don't feel like getting wet and bothered for nothing.

And my options are low, because I don't date non-blacks.

And really, its not even about race. It's about getting with someone who is mature enough to build with me, rather than tear me down, with foolishness and mess.

And I just haven't found anyone who is worthy of my time, or attention.

Like I said, I spend almost every waking hour, of my day, trying to find viable work that can pay the rent, and give me excess, for savings.

I am not hardly thinking about dating.

Do You Want To Marry A Rich Man?

No. Not really. But I don't want him to be poor either.

But I really only want to marry, if we can keep our own names, and finances separate.

I don't want to marry for name, or joined purse. I am so against that!

Where Is Home For You, In the USA?

I guess I call that place, New York, now. I mean, I have lived here, the longest. I have been in New York since Oct of 2000. So I have lived here almost 15 or 16 years.

And I lived in Houston from 1983-85, and from-1995-2000. So that would be my second home.

And Iowa, I was there for a few years, under five. But that was for Foster Care, and "immigration processing", as I call it.

So yeah, here in the United States, I consider New York, my home.

And I bet I would absolutely love it here, if I had my own housing, and money! Whoo-hoot!

We Saw All Of Your Lawsuits, Especially The One Against Beyoncé, and Kim Kardashian. What do you have to say about that?

All I have to say about those lawsuits is this. I was search in the dark for a solution to my problem. And based on the information I had, or didn't have, at the time, I felt the need to petition those people, for relief, and solution, to some of the issues I faced.

What Issues Did You Face That Would Cause You to Sue Beyoncé and Kim?

Financial. Laugh. Ha-ha.

I know that got a riser out of you!

No. But. Really, I felt led, or motivated to petition Kim, Beyonce, and a whole host of others, for the same reason – Human Traffick.

Now, I am not saying Kim, or Beyonce's daughters are "Trafficked", but I am saying, I felt led to petition them.

The problem is that, we have a mutual contact. And, that individual was involved in Human Trafficking. Or at least they have an associate, they know, who does it.

So, in my ignorance, I called myself petitioning those people, not realizing that there are media outlets, waiting for "opportunities", to bring petitions, like mine, forward – for purposes of exploitation.

And that is exactly what they did.

And, what is so horrible about the one, to Beyonce, is that, I asked the Judge, infamous, Judge Preska, to seal the file. And she disregarded my request.

I don't think she even entertained it at all.

And then come to find out, after judicial reprimand, of her, and judicial review, of a higher court, she was unjustified in the way she handled my petitions, before SDNY.

She operated in extreme bias, because I didn't understand legal language, or wasn't competent, at the time, to write it.

If you must know, I petitioned Beyonce, and Kim, because I believed, they might have received one of my eggs, through in vitro.

And instead of asking the court for a DNA test, of their children, I attempted to mask that, bit of info, thinking SDNY, the holder of the RICO matter, associated with that case, knew what I was asking for.

But, again, that was ignorance on my part.

Because I had no idea, that Beyonce, or Kim, were media targets like that. And I had no idea that a petition, filed, in court, would come to the news like that.

I was completely ignorant to that.

But the thing is, I don't know Beyonce or Kim personally. And it's not like I would go to one of their events, and attempt to speak to them, about anything.

So in the United States, the way to contact someone who is famous, or otherwise, that you don't know, is to Civil Serve them. And so I served them, to ask them a question.

And the question was, "Did you use in vitro, to conceive your daughter?"

Or, "Was your daughter born from a surrogate? At 22-27 weeks, during April of 2012?"

Or, if you have discovered, that your child, possesses my DNA, can we negotiate a deal, so I can give you permission, for using my DNA, without my consent, or knowledge.

That was the whole premise for all of my lawsuits.

And I realize that my handwriting looked a bit strange. But there are few things you have to understand.

First of all, and I keep saying this, SDNY, is an Administrative Court. Which means, you never really see a judge.

Strange Questions, Even Stranger Answers
Written by Prophetess Tina Seals

Your petition goes before you, before the judge. And if your legal language is not good enough, as a Pro Se Litigant, you most times, don't get past the first review, of your petition.

So it's very high pressure for me. I mean, I try and get everything into the little form they give you. But sometimes, while you are in the SDNY office, you forget what you want to say, legally, and otherwise.

You are often times under pressure to place your petition in the office, before a certain time, and it's just really high pressure.

Because as a pro se litigant, you don't have the legal knowledge you need to even feel successful, in the court – unless it's just an all-out win situation – for you. Meaning, like a "summary judgment", kind of thing.

And legally, I knew my situations, to be that.

Everyone I petitioned, should have had the legal right to do a deal with me, under the Equal Protection Clause of the 5th, and 14th amendments, despite the fact that the larger matter, governing the cases, and defendants, was a RICO/Terrorism question.

But again, Judge Preska, the Honorable Judge Preska, dismissed everything, with prejudice, except my most recent filing.

She didn't let me do deals with any of the defendants, or their clients.

Citing you can't, "make deals with terrorist!"

And I guess, legally, what she is saying is, they, the federal government, considers the people responsible, for the exploited DNA, terrorist.

I don't know if they have been legally declared to be "terrorist", or not.

But if not, that was an illegal move on her part. Because she cannot refuse them Habeas Corpus, unless they are awaiting trial for capital murder, standing trial for a gross crime against humanity, or declared by the federal government, to be a terrorist.

And if they were any of those, they would most likely be in a maximum security facility.

None of these, nor myself, are any of those.

So, I didn't think it strange to ask Beyonce or Kim that question.

Nor did I think it strange to ask them for compensation, for the use of my exploited DNA, because it was done without my knowledge, consent, and compensation.

I guarantee you Kim, and Beyonce, both, would petition me, if I used their DNA, without consent, and compensation.

So I didn't do anything they wouldn't have done.

But I get why she probably didn't want to let me pursue them in court. Because it would have revealed their contacts.

There had to be a doctor who removed the babies. And there was clearly a hospital or other facility that incubated. Unless they used midwives, and home incubating units, with visiting nurses.

I don't know.

But what I didn't like, was that she allowed Beyonce, Kim, and the others to be exploited. I didn't like that.

And what I mean by that is, she should have sealed, or scrubbed the petitions, so that they couldn't be accessed.

She knew the deal. She knew they were high profile. And she knew I was a homeless lady, living in a mica shelter. Which stands for Mentally Ill, Chemically Defendent.

So she knew I didn't have any money to seal the file. And she also knew I didn't have any way of contacting the Defendants, without civilly petitioning them in court.

If I were her, and I am not a lawyer, yet, I would have sealed the records. And because of the inflammatory nature of the petitions, insinuating, their kids are trafficked, or the DNA used to create them, was trafficked, I would have asked for a conference of the parties, and a DNA test, to find out.

So she, the judge, in essence, wanted to embarrass me, and them. And she, no doubt, did a great job of humiliating me, by dismissing all but my current petition, as frivolous.

I'm just grateful she didn't hinder their careers.

I petitioned because I wanted to spare them the embarrassment, of having to do one of these NY Subway Trafficked Kids Trials.

Anyway. So that was why I petitioned.

I don't know Beyonce, or Kim. And I am not about to go to any of their events and try and speak with them.

So I petitioned them in civil court, to speak to them, about the issue.

And everyone, who is legal minded, understands, I didn't care to speak to Beyonce, and Kim, per se, just a legal representative, who could work out the deal with me, and spare them embarrassment, and make the issue go away.

That's all.

But no. The judge mishandled the cases. She didn't let me proceed with them, but yet they got published. Hum, that sounds curious to me. Sounds like she wanted them to be embarrassed.

Listen, understand, she had to let that case be entered into the record. I didn't have the power to do that myself.

So Why Did You Sue the Churches? Including Your Own?

For the same reason. The Human Traffick. I got the idea that if I petitioned the local pastors, and asked them for names of trafficked kids, that I would do a deal with their parents, for the illegal use of my DNA.

And I wasn't looking to gain anything from those populations. Most of them are poor, and cant pay. This is especially true in the minority churches.

This, I believe, was why they elected to take these trafficked kids, many of them. I think they thought they could get citizenship, child support, welfare, food stamps, or other financial incentives, for having these kids.

But it didn't work out that way.

Because the problem with that is, there are laws against the illegal use of someone's DNA, in the United States.

You cannot force someone to become a parent, by creating a child, with their egg, and then bringing it to them.

IT doesn't work that way.

And because they didn't know the law, they thought, only DNA evidence, that the birth mother existed, would force the hand of the court, to provide the families of these children, with compensation.

It doesn't work that way.

Having children is about "pro-choice", not "pro-force".

If it were "pro-force", can you imagine the numbers of people, who would be forced into parenthood, by Human Traffickers? Wow.

And the second issue is, when you meet someone, you meet them, based on how they introduce themselves.

If you introduce me to your child, and call her Lynn, then I will forever know "Lynn", as your child.

I have no reason to suspect Lynn to be my child.

First of all, I didn't meet Lynn in the womb. Nor did I sleep with Lynn's father. So why would I ever think Lynn to be my child?

And greater, even if I did sleep with the father, if I terminated the pregnancy, I chose to end life. Why should I expect a child, that I legally terminated, under the law, to show up, and expect me to mother them, some odd 20 years later?

Sounds like malpractice to me!

So by petitioning the churches, I thought I would be able to get a list of names, of these children. Then I would do a deal with each of the parents of these children, to show the court, that I was compensated, something, as a result of my forced, and illegal DNA use.

The whole point, was to spare them legal liability.

But again, Judge Preska, wouldn't allow me to do deals, with the people who had the kids.

Because think about it, to do a deal with those people, is to reduce the amount of children left, who need to be litigated, as evidence, on the part of the traffickers.

So if James trafficked 100 of those kids, or sold DNA, to 100 clients, and I did a deal with all of his clients, he wouldn't have legal liability.

I would have done a contractual agreement, with his customers, giving them retro permission, to use my EGG, on my terms, with mutually agreed upon, compensation.

That was my sole objective.

But when the system, wants to deprive you of equity, and justice, under the Law, they deny you the right to exercise your legal right to contract, in such settings.

And really, as far as I am concerned, the RICO matter, and my deals, with the Defendants, clients, had nothing to do with one another.

They are their clients, but they trafficked my DNA. If I chose to do a deal with their clients, then that is my business.

I should be able to be compensated for my efforts. And to also grant permission to those I chose to allow to carry my DNA.

What Is My Professional Relationship With PFC?

None. I am not a leader, organizer, minister, or any other legal, authorized, or binding representative of PFC, at this time.

Nor do I anticipate being such.

PFC is a qualified ministry. They have established leadership. And to my knowledge, are not looking for my assistance, in any area of service to that ministry.

Smile.

What Is My Relationship With The Leadership of PFC?

Professional.

Thank You for Reading

Thank you for taking the time to read this book. It is my prayer that it has been helpful to you.

If you are interested in reading other books that I have written, you can find them online at Amazon, Create Space, or Barnes and Noble.

Should you feel so inclined you can drop me an email at seals_tina@yahoo.com, or at tina@tinaseals.com, or tina@tinaseals.net.

Strange Questions, Even Stranger Answers
Written by Prophetess Tina Seals

Your past, present, and future support of this ministry, is greatly needed, and appreciated.

Jesus Bless you –

Prophetess Tina Seals

www.ingramcontent.com/pod-product-compliance
Lightning Source LLC
Chambersburg PA
CBHW070959180526
45168CB00003B/1218